YOUR KNOWLEDGE HAS VALUE

Muddasir Malik

KHMRAJ - Hierarchy Method of Teaching

GRIN Verlag

Bibliografische Information der Deutschen Nationalbibliothek:

Die Deutsche Bibliothek verzeichnet diese Publikation in der Deutschen National-
bibliografie; detaillierte bibliografische Daten sind im Internet über http://dnb.d-
nb.de/ abrufbar.

Imprint:

Copyright © 2013 GRIN Verlag GmbH
Druck und Bindung: Books on Demand GmbH, Norderstedt Germany
ISBN: 978-3-656-34676-0

This book at GRIN:

http://www.grin.com/en/e-book/207211/khmraj-hierarchy-method-of-teaching

KHMRAJ HIERARCHY METHOD OF TEACHING

Abstract:

We have gone through different methods of teaching but the advantages of one method become the limitations of other method. Keeping in view this, we have prepared a new hierarchy method of teaching called" KHMRAJ HIERARCHY METHOD OF TEACHING. It includes these steps in sequence, Dalton division, preparation, lecture/presentation, buzz group, discussion, brainstorming, problem, projects, and seminar method. This hierarchy method will definitely bring some positive modification in our present system of education.

Key Words:- Teaching method, hierarchy, lecture, discussion, projects, seminar

Introduction

The KHMRAJ hierarchy method of teaching is prepared by Muddasir Hamid Malik of Department of Education, University of Kashmir 2012. We know that method is the instrument in the hands of a teacher through which a complex subject matter can be easily understood by any learner. No doubt we have passed through different methods of teaching that have influenced the educational systems of different countries at different times. Every teacher whether in primary, secondary or tertiary level have acquainted themselves with different methods of teachings and possesses knowledge that how different methods serves our educational system at different points. The teachers while entering into the classroom think whether lecture, discussion, role playing, problem solving, project method etc. should be used in the classroom. He thinks that if I will use lecture method, the advantages of other methods will become limitations of my classroom and likely he thinks about other methods. He remains in a dilemma and enters into class without preparing his topic according to the guidelines of any teaching method. He teaches in the classroom haphazardly and this results into wastage in terms of time, energy, money etc. The teachers always use specific methods of teaching for a particular content and the drawbacks or the advantages of other methods acts as limitations.

The whole process of education according to modern psychology revolves around the learner that means everything should be child-centred. Learner's role is considered as pivotal because he is the agent for whom the whole process is meant for. The different specific teaching methods used by the teachers at specific times for specific contents no doubt brings change to some extent but overall the progress of learners remains standstill due to different reasons. Modern child-centred education has diminished the role of teacher and highlighted learner as more important than teacher. The teacher who was in ancient India considered as Guru have been put behind the curtain because of the modern teaching methodology but this KHMRAJ hierarchy method of teaching neither keeps the teacher behind the curtain nor neglects the student's importance in the process of teaching and learning and keeps both active as well as alive in the classroom. This KHMRAJ hierarchy method of teaching will overcome the shortcomings of most methods of teachings and will incorporate the advantages of different methods of teachings. No teacher will now think that which method of teaching should we use or choose for teaching a particular topic. After acquainting himself with this KHMRAJ hierarchy method of teaching, the teachers will not be dependent upon other methods of teachings simply by going through the procedure of this method. Now the teachers need not to worry that which method will they use in the classroom for teaching a particular topic.

This KHMRAJ hierarchy method of teaching will bring some positive changes both among teachers as well as students. The students after reading any topic through this method of teaching will definitely bring something positive in their career as resourceful ones. They will be able to generate new ideas, thoughts and creative expressions. The students will become socially efficient ones by taking part in different projects that will be completed in social environment. The teachers will also think along different lines and may generate new ideas and concepts that will be definitely utilitarian in nature (INSHA ALLAH).

This hierarchy method of teaching will work in those classes where only 4 or 5 lectures will be delivered a day. It will be most useful at the tertiary level of education. The whole procedure through which this method will work are as:

a) **Dalton division:** This is the beginning of this hierarchy method of teaching. In this phase, as the session will start in the institutions, the teachers will prepare the detailed outlines of their syllabi. The syllabus of each subject will be divided into half month units. Each unit should have complete directions and references for study so that the students too may come prepared for the next topic and content. The teachers will be called subject teachers or specialists having specialization in particular papers not class teachers like philosophy teacher, psychology teacher etc. The whole library including laboratory will be divided according to their respective subject rooms so that the subject teacher or learner whenever during discussion phase needs any help should consult them easily at their hand. These rooms should be called subject rooms instead of classrooms. All the subject rooms should be labeled as per their respective subjects.

b) **preparation:**

Preparation is considered as the base of any planning. Unless and until we will not make good preparation for plan, that plan will not yield better results. The KHMRAJ hierarchy method of teaching will start with the preparation phase. This phase will be preparation for both the teacher as well as for the students. The teacher will select the content that he is going to present before the students. Before presenting the content, the teacher will collect all the relevant material that will be helpful and related directly or indirectly to the content that a teacher is going to present before the students. He will collect the relevant material from books, journals, references, e-contents etc. in order to make his lesson more and more qualitative or in other words to make the topic or content more and more resourceful (because I have personal experience that our teachers teach that content which they have taught 5 years ago, there was no up-to-date information regarding the contents which they have taught us. They prepared notes five years ago and till this date, I have not seen any change in those notes, the change of 'is' have not been found anywhere in those notes or in that material). One more duty of teacher will be that, he will tell the students in advance that tomorrow we are going to study that particular topic or content and be prepared for that topic. He will also tell them in advance that there will be no restrictions in discussing any question or issue related to our topic.

c) **Lecture/presentation:**

Before presenting the content in the subjectroom, the teacher will initiate the topic by asking some relevant questions regarding the topic in order to capture the attention of the students(the use of *question-answer method*). Taking one of the questions as an initiator of the topic, the teacher will now start presenting his topic before the students. During his lecture/presentation, he may use the different audio-visual aids, charts, maps etc. that may be appropriate according to the topic to be learnt. He may use different illustrations for explaining different concepts, ideas and objects in the subjectroom (*illustration method*). During the presentation/lecture, he may also use demonstration to enable them to learn skills and get concept clarified. The teacher may explain the concept theoretically and then through demonstration may actually show how the different parts of a concept work practically (*demonstration method*). It depends upon the topic that whether the teacher will only explain theoretically or give demonstration also. The teacher should use at least two languages viz., regional or mother tongue and English (for those whose mother tongue is English should only use English language) for presenting the content so that the learners will achieve or retain the topic easily (because our rural population which comprises of 70% does not know English as medium of instruction, they understand better through mother tongue or regional language). Presenting any content or topic before students has some definite objectives behind that and one of the main objective of teaching is that students should learn something, thus by presenting the content, in Indian context, in regional or mother tongue will definitely lead students towards progress in terms of content or topic. The teacher should also use teaching skills during his lecture/presentation of the content so that the learners may remain attentive during the whole classroom teaching-learning situation.

d) **Buzz-group:**

In this phase, the teacher will divide the whole class into small groups (5-8) called team groups. The teacher will divide them into different small groups on the basis of certain procedures like by assigning them to different groups on the basis of intelligence, individual differences that means equal distribution of individuals into different groups. Every team group will be headed by a team leader. This division will be done mainly for the purpose of channelizing students' energy constructively.

e) **Discussion:**

After dividing the class into small team groups, the discussion phase comes into play. The team groups will discuss the topic or content as lectured/presented by the teacher in the classroom. This phase is completed in an atmosphere of freedom, spontaneity and democracy is maintained throughout the discussion by the teacher. Now here, the teacher acts as an observer who continuously observes and records their discussion points. The team group members also note down the different points that they will discuss during this phase. The members of the different team groups will take the pros and cons of the topic. During discussion, they will differentiate, compare and contrast the current topic with another one that will be suitable for this purpose. They will also discuss its advantages and limitations. This all will be done under the supervision of the concerned class teacher. The teacher will also help them in this discussion wherever the need arises. They will wholly and solely discuss the lesson taught by the teacher.

f) **Brain-storming:**

In this phase, the team group members will express their creative ideas. They will now provide their own view points or ideas that will be useful for them. The criticism made by them in the discussion phase is now replied or answered by team members on behalf of their leader in the presence of the teacher. This is the phase which will also give rise to different problems that will be later on taken as projects. Here the teacher will also try to solve those problems or issues raised during discussion session. Some problems or issues will remain unsolved and they will become the topics for projects.

g) **Problem:**

In this phase, the students will now choose the problems as raised in the brain-storming phase. The problems will be of educational significance related to their curriculum which will arise during the above phase. These problems will be the issues or difficulties raised during the above phase.

h) **Projects:**

Actually this phase will start at any time during the completion of the said course. The problems should be assigned to different team members in the form of projects according to their individual differences. The important point here we will bring into notice is that projects should be compulsory for every team member. The students do not show interest towards these projects where ever they are being certified with total grade, so we want to introduce the separate certificates for these projects. A separate certificate should be given to the students for these projects. A student without this certificate should not be eligible for any post for recruitment.

These projects will be chosen separately or as a group project *(group or individual projects)*. They will work on those projects in laboratory conditions or will complete them in the field. For science students, they may use heurism *(heuristic method)* for the completion of their projects. These projects will be done under the supervision of their respective subject teachers.

i) **Seminar:**

The last phase of this method will be the seminar *(seminar method)*. According to the English author Francis Bacon, "reading makes the full man, writing the exact man and conference the ready man". The seminars will be held at the end of the course. The different problems that the individual students will take as their projects will be defended in the seminars in the form of paper readings followed by discussion regarding those problems that raised during the course lectured/presented and whether those problems have been solved or not. The audience will critically examine the paper and will discuss the content or findings of the paper in the light of the problem or project taken. This is the way through which the students will develop their wholesome personality and may be able to generate new ideas and concepts.

This KHMRAJ hierarchy method of teaching includes:

- *Dalton plan*

- *Lecture method*

- *Question-answer method*

- *Demonstration method*

- *Illustration method*

- *Buzz-group*

- *Discussion method*

- *Brain-storming method*

- *Project method*

- *Heuristic method and*

- *Seminar method of teaching.*